Unravelings

Unravelings

Sarah Cheshire

Etchings Press
Indianapolis, Indiana
2017

This publication is made possible by the funding provided by the College of Arts and Sciences and the English Department at the University of Indianapolis. Special thanks to IngramSpark and to those students who judged, edited, designed, and published this chapbook: Kylie Seitz, Mercadees Hempel, and Natalie McCann.

University *of* INDIANAPOLIS.

Published by Etchings Press
1400 E. Hanna Ave.
Indianapolis, IN 46227

etchings.uindy.edu
www.uindy.edu/cas/english

Printed by IngramSpark
www.ingramspark.com/

Published in the United States of America

ISBN 978-0-9988976-3-9

23 22 21 20 19 18 17   3 4 5
Third Printing, June 2019

Prologue
Storytelling as Grey Matter

What does it mean to dwell in the spaces between lines? How is ambiguity both a necessary and authentic creative device and a potentially dangerous impediment to artistic accountability?

In crafting this narrative, my intention is not to seek retribution or cast blame, but to delve into the intricate psychological landscape of a relationship imbued in both intimate creative energy and deep power imbalance. Through my own story, I hope to issue a larger interrogation of how we as storytellers construct and reconstruct truth through narrative and the ways in which accountability can become complicated through our manipulations of memory, both those advertent and those inadvertent.

The Title IX deposition in this piece is my own creative work. It is an attempt to recreate a complex situation through a removed perspective and neither reflects nor draws from official documents.

Names, places, and certain other identifying markers have been obscured to respect the privacy of characters.

Two months and two days after my college graduation, I find myself sitting in a large armchair in the office of the campus Title IX Coordinator. All of my friends have long moved back to their bustling East Coast cities to embark on prestigious unpaid internships, and I am somehow still stuck in post-grad limbo, here in the cornfields of my small midwestern college town.

I trace my initials in sweat across the leather armrests and watch the markings fade into the crimson. My throat feels like it has been coated in chalk. Sunlight pulses from the oversized window across the left side of my face like a mild dose of electroshock-therapy. I blink.

The woman in front of me scribbles the date on her notepad and repositions her swivel chair so that she is facing me. She has an eyebrow piercing and a gentle laugh, both of which make me want to divulge to her, even though I know I should be careful. She smiles and furrows her brow:

"We can go completely at your own pace."

I blink again. I am still trying to fill in the gaps from the night before—

~~

I remember getting drinks at the local bar with the Dean of Students and some "people he wanted me to meet." *Networking* or some such bizarre ritual of young adulthood. I remember rounds and rounds of gin and tonics

3

and, sometime in the blur, approaching the bar for more—

A man with a backwards baseball cap, eyes that slid past my face and down my body a beat too quickly—

Down down down

What else? A grab, maybe a grope; a flinch, maybe a snarl—

I remember how I pulled away, how he wouldn't relent—

How his lips drew tight lines around his teeth and how spit sprayed from his mouth when he talked—

Did he call me *bitch*? Or was it *slut*? Or is my memory drawing from someplace else, someplace further back?

No, it was one of these words. I remember because of the way my reflexes sprung into autopilot—

A riptide, raging through the space below my ribcage,

Fine china shattering down from rows of shelves under my skin—

It's a familiar feeling,

I am standing flat-footed on solid ground. Someone switches a flip. The breath gets sucked out of me. My mind goes blank—

fuck

How hard did I push him?

Something clattered. Someone gasped.

Unravelings

From the Desk of Title IX Coordinator O.

Preliminary Notes
Investigation into Misconduct Report Against X., Professor of Creative Writing
July 31, 2014

On the morning of July 31th, 2014 Dean S. of the College of Arts and Sciences reported obtaining information from a recent college graduate ("Jane Doe") regarding a potential prohibited relationship between herself and Professor X., of the Department of Creative Writing, which transpired throughout the 2013–2014 academic year.

Jane Doe was subsequently called into the Title IX Office to discuss this information.

It is noted that Jane Doe, according to Dean S., "inadvertently" disclosed this information and is tentative about pursuing an investigation (she has expressed to the Title IX office a desire "not to get anyone in trouble"). Nevertheless, in compliance with the college's Sexual Offense Policy (revised May 2013) and Federal Title IX mandates, this office is required to investigate these claims to ensure that the institution as a whole remains a safe learning environment for students.

Hereby, in accordance to Doe's testimony, this office is opening an investigation into the conduct of Professor X., seeking to establish whether his actions throughout the 2013–2014 academic year were in violation of:

a.) The college's sexual harassment policy,
b.) Federal Title IX laws,
c.) The college's faculty conduct and sexual offense policy, which strictly prohibits relationship between faculty members and students.

Furthermore, The Title IX Office wishes to investigate the degree to which the Creative Writing Department was complicit in the perpetuation of any misconduct that may have transpired during the 2013–2014 academic year.

The swivel chair squeaks on the hardwood floor. I pluck a withered piece of romaine lettuce out of my bangs and start to roll it between my thumb and index finger, then remember that the woman is still watching me:

"I don't want anyone to get I trouble." I stuff the little green lettuce ball into the upholstery of the armchair.

~~

I remember the bartender with the dragon sleeve tattoos puffing his chest, "Calm down! Everyone calm down."

Everyone. Calm. Down.

EveryoneCalmDown

Everyone—

Everyone is clustered around me: the Dean, some professor who once did a guest lecture on Imposter Syndrome in my Intro Psych class, his wife, all the shiny networkers in freshly ironed clothes whom I am supposed to be impressing. X-raying me. My mascara skid-marking my cheeks. *Bitch*. My little blue dress revealing what I now realize is too much skin. *Slut.*

I remember goosebumps, pale blue—

How my legs looked like ghosts.

I can still feel the clammy chill of his hand against my thigh. The sensation it leaves behind is strange and invasive but also familiar—

My heart is pounding.

Suddenly this is no longer about the asshole sprawled

out across the table in front of me, clutching his wrist and groaning. It is not just about this one grope. It is about all the unwanted touches, which are now surfacing from underneath my skin with a force almost beyond my control. It is about the acute feeling that I don't really exist, that I am just a construction of unwanted touches, a molding of the places Their Hands have grasped. I am unwanted touch upon unwanted touch upon unwanted touch upon hands upon hands upon cold, clammy hands—

I am back in His kitchen, sometime in mid-December. Red ink marked papers are scattered across the dining room table. He is pressed against me. We are pressed together. I know I shouldn't be there, but there is something thrilling about how the boundary between us is growing murkier and murkier as he takes a step closer. How we are flipping the script that says that he is Powerful and I am Vulnerable... because I want to be here just as much as he does, right?

I remember tracing my fingers across his clavicle in figure eights, my back pressed into the stove door—

How his hands felt sandpaper: not really in a bad way, but maybe not in a good way either—

Did he initiate the kiss or did I?

I know I should keep this touch tucked away, but it has been growing more and more potent throughout the past seven months since he started subtly changing my final grades, pausing his hand over mine in advising meetings, avoiding my eyes in public spaces, reeling me into secret meetings in Places Where They Surely Won't See Us, and showing me beautifully harrowing excerpts from his yet-to-be-published anthology—

Stories about his home country and the ghosts that still followed him.

Over the past seven months, I have found myself wavering indeterminately between *Am I Crazy* and *Is This Love*—

I have kept telling myself that maybe my power is a space somewhere in between, that maybe if only I tried a little harder I could get there. *I could tame the ghosts*—

Or would the ghosts creep up on me?

It is so close to the surface now, this touch—

Am I crazy?

~~

I wake up with a sore wrist and my face buried in my leftover salad.

~~

How much did I share?

~~

The woman in the swivel chair takes two rolls of Smarties from a ceramic bowl on her desk, hands me one. I love Smarties. Fuck. She's got me cornered. She crinkles open the wrapper and pops an orange candy into her mouth:

"Why don't you tell me a little bit about what happened—between you and Professor X.?"

From the Desk of Title IX Coordinator O.

Preliminary Notes
Investigation into Misconduct Report Against X., Professor of Creative Writing
July 31, 2014

Timeline of Events, According to Jane Doe's Initial Testimony

September, 2013: Jane Doe solicits Professor X. to advise her senior Creative Writing thesis, which is to be in the genre of Creative Nonfiction.

Early October, 2013: Jane Doe and two other Creative Writing students learn of Professor X.'s impending departure from the college due to the limited terms of his teaching fellowship. Under Doe's leadership, the students create and disseminate an online petition to procure a tenure track faculty position for Professor X., citing both Professor X.'s "immense skills as a teacher" and the need for the college to "retain more faculty members of color." The petition soon goes viral, attracting over 500 signatures from students, alumni, parents, and a handful of faculty, the most assertive of whom is Professor E., chair of the Creative Writing Department. Professor X., Doe reports, remains "only peripherally involved" in this initiative, wanting it to remain "a grassroots student movement." However, he allegedly continuously feeds Doe information about appropriate outlets through which to channel her organizing.

Mid October, 2013: Doe is contacted by multiple campus newspapers to discuss the small "student movement" she has found herself leading on Professor X.'s behalf. She starts meeting with college administrators to discuss strategic planning for the creation of this tenure track position.

Late October, 2013: Doe and Professor X. allegedly start spending "more and more time" together, discussing both her writing and the "politics surrounding the petition." At Professor X.'s recommendation, they start holding their meetings at a 'secret location' (the table in the back of an East Asian Grocery Store). Doe allegedly feels her senior thesis meetings becoming "more intimate," as she begins to explore "personal topics related to the body memory and violence" in her creative work. Professor X. allegedly expresses a "profound investment in supporting [Doe] and helping [her] tell [her] story." He conveys "his solidarity and support" by sharing intimate details of his own personal history with Doe—which he claims "never to have told a student before," ~~including information about a late~~

~~family member who allegedly died from a virus she contracted after being sexually assaulted~~ [information retracted at Doe's request].

Professor X. taught me the power of non-linear narrative.

We talked about this in October of 2013, in his office in the upstairs room of the little stone house on College Street, home to the campus Creative Writing Department. I was struggling to write my senior thesis. He was my advisor.

I remember how he started this meeting off, by asking me how my mother was doing. He asked this regularly at the beginnings of meetings. It was one of the many quirks that made him both charming and intriguing.

"She's doing alright, thanks," I said, even though the last time I had talked to my mother she had been humming under her breath and talking nonsensically about her fears that my stepdad was leading a double life as a pirate. "How is your mother?"

"Fine," he said, "wonderful in fact! In good health. Enjoying her crossword puzzles. Drinking enough brandy to keep her spirits up. Thank you for asking."

~~

On that day in October, I was having a hard time figuring out where to begin with my writing. I was trying to tell a certain story, something that still felt a bit raw and muddled inside me. Every time I would sit down to write, the words would get stuck. This wasn't a story with a clear beginning, middle, or end. The most important parts had been lost in my memory; maybe due to alcohol, or selective memory, or the way my mind goes blank sometimes in moments of

panic—
Does this sound familiar?

From the Desk of Title IX Coordinator O.

Continuation of Timeline of Events, According to Jane Doe's Initial Testimony

Early November, 2013: Doe walks into the Creative Writing Building one afternoon to hand in an assignment. She allegedly finds Professor X. and Professor E. (Creative Writing Department chair), discussing her petition. Professor E. tells her to stay, recommends that the three of them continue the conversation in the privacy of her off-campus house (according to Doe, Professor E. later professes a suspicion that the Creative Writing Building is being 'bugged' by the college administration). At her house, Professor E. gives Doe and Professor X. "multiple beers." Professor E. and Professor X. allegedly "start to gossip" with Doe about college faculty personnel drama, which they feel, according to Professor E., could obstruct the creation of a tenure track position for Professor X. This includes feelings that Dean S. and Title IX Coordinator O. harbor a longwithstanding "animosity" towards Professor X. and should not be trusted. Professor E. allegedly tells Doe that she is giving her this information to help "inform her student organizing." Urges Doe to "be careful with whom she discusses" matters related to Professor X. and her petition. Professor E. then drives Doe to her Creative Writing pedagogy class, where she arrives "late and slightly inebriated."

Mid November, 2013: Doe receives a series of Facebook messages from Professor E. under a profile guised as a "picture of a cat wearing sunglasses." In these messages, Professor E. relays confidential information to Doe regarding potential sources of funding that have started to open for Professor X.'s tenure track position, pushback from [unnamed] faculty members, and increasing internal tension within the Creative Writing Department. Professor E. allegedly reminds Doe that many "higher ups" are not to be trusted; urges her to a create a private (non-college affiliated) email address for further clandestine communications. Doe reports "beginning to feel slightly paranoid" but also being "flattered to have older mentors demonstrating such trust" in her.

Fwd: Not sure   Inbox   x

▬▬▬▬▬▬▬▬▬▬▬▬▬▬@gmail.com>   11/6/13

to me, ▬▬▬▬▬▬▬▬

The email address thing gets confusing, I realize. Sarah, I have been sending stuff to your ▬▬▬ email that seems okay because it's not specifically about "strategizing"--
(i.e., "plotting") -- pertaining to the petition and college policy stuff... but more confidential stuff I'll continue to send to your gmail address. There's an arbitratriness about
the definition of "more confidential"--

[Collection of Evidence]

Mid November, 2013: As secret meetings continue, Doe begins to sense "a strong underlying [romantic] tension between Professor X. and [herself]." Reports feeling that this tension is "mutual" but nonetheless being concerned that it might affect her ability to advocate for Professor X. in as objective and conscientious a manner as possible.

Mid November, 2013: Doe and Professor X. have Thanksgiving Dinner at Professor E.'s house. Allegedly get "slightly inebriated" [reliable memory?] and continue to discuss college personal/ personnel issues in depth. Around 12:30 AM, Doe and Professor X. allegedly walk home together. According to Doe, they end up sitting on the fire escape behind the hospital, where Doe approaches Professor X. about the "tensions" she has been perceiving. Professor X. allegedly responds that his feelings for her are "more than merely pedestrian." They allegedly hold hands.

A few days before Thanksgiving, the snow starts falling. It comes down light and steady at first, cloaking the town in a thin white gown. Throughout the next days, we watch from the dorm windows as the flakes continue to fall, the white dunes outside silently thickening—

This winter will soon go down history as one of the coldest on record in this small midwestern town. Over the next five months, this snow will become buried under new layers, which will turn from white to ashen grey to white to grey over and over before the grass is once again visible.

On the day before Thanksgiving however, the snow still drapes the earth as a beautiful, shimmering gown; untarnished in its newness and its stark silent whiteness.

~~

Sometime after midnight on Thanksgiving, Professor X. and I make our way back from Professor E.'s house, our bellies brimming with pumpkin pie and butternut squash soup: a recipe handed down from someone's mother—

I trip into a snowbank. Professor X. offers an arm. I notice how small white crystals cling to his eyelashes—

The streets are silent except for the low hum of streetlamps, straining their light through forcefields of ice. Most students have gone home for break. Those who remain are huddled inside the houses and buildings, wrapped in the warmth of sleep.

We stumble through the streets, almost weightlessly:

Our skin buzzing from bubbly white wine, our feet intercepted midstep by cushions of snow.

The landscape is as smooth as the surface of a pearl, except for the single jagged row of craters carved by our footprints—

I imagine this is how the astronauts felt when they first stepped onto the face of the moon:

Freefalling through the monosyllabic whiteness of a space they thought they knew but had only really seen from a distance—

Staring out into an emptiness, both exhilarating and dangerous in its lack of limits—

~~

[Disquiet: a word he would always scrawl on the pages of my stories, describing the sensation of mutedness; like the grazing of a hand over thinly veiled flesh, or a scream muffled into a pillow, or a memory that has no words, maybe a body tumbling in slow motion through a space unbound by gravity, or the soft roar one might hear if one amplified the sound of an eyelash fluttering—]

~~

We pause behind the hospital, him leaning against the railing of the fire escape, me standing in his elongated shadow—

I notice how his words leave a ghost-like vapor in the air as they fall from his mouth:

"My feelings for you are more than merely pedestrian."

I am taken aback by the poignancy of this word: *pedestrian*.

It's only later that I realize that I have no idea what precisely it means.

From the Desk of Title IX Coordinator O.

Mid November, 2013: Doe and Professor X. allegedly exchange a series of "intimate text messages" [potential evidence?].

Early December, 2013: Doe and Professor X. allegedly drive together off campus in Doe's car. ~~According to Doe, this is the anniversary of Professor X.'s sister's death, and every year he goes to get tested for HIV "to honor her memory and to celebrate his own life." This year, he has invited Doe to accompany him in this commemoration~~ [information redacted at Doe's request]. They allegedly take only backroads; Professor X. is worried that "people might see [them] together and raise eyebrows." They stop for beers at a "small dive bar" outside of town, where they hold hands and engage in "intimate conversation." On their drive home, Professor X. allegedly confesses to Doe that he has been "weighing the potential risks of [them] starting an affair."

I later found out that his mother was dead. She had been dead for sixteen years, along with his father. Her of tuberculosis, him of malaria. Or maybe vice versa? He had spent his teen years floating between the homes of aunts and uncles and teachers and family friends, trying to remember without remembering, trying to solicit help without asking—through a smile, maybe, or a compliment, or an astute observation, such as the ones he would make about me. "Do you realize, Sarah, that whenever you are thinking about things that you do not yet have the words for, you laugh twice?"

He learned to be charismatic, cunning with words, to charm his way into spaces that might otherwise be off limits—

At the age of sixteen, he was accepted to study at one of the most prestigious public boarding schools in his home country.

When he spoke of his mother, he was really speaking of an aid worker from Massachusetts who had helped him apply to college in The States. A slender, sandy-haired woman who enjoyed crossword puzzles and always took her supper with a glass of brandy.

He told me this in secret, during a midnight walk in which we had subconsciously gravitated into the shadows of academic buildings: "I do not want to be pitied, you see."

I immediately wondered why he had lied to me and, what's more, why he had set himself up for this lie. When he asked me about my mother, he must have known I would echo the question back to him, right?

I wasn't angry with him, just confused. I told myself that maybe he was only deviating from the truth by a nuance; what's the difference, really, between a mother and someone who fulfills a maternal role?

~~

Maybe this is the power of storytelling, right?

To twist words around, to explain away absences: reframe. To make sense out of senselessness. To write mothers into motherlessness. Maybe to convince, maybe to unconvince—

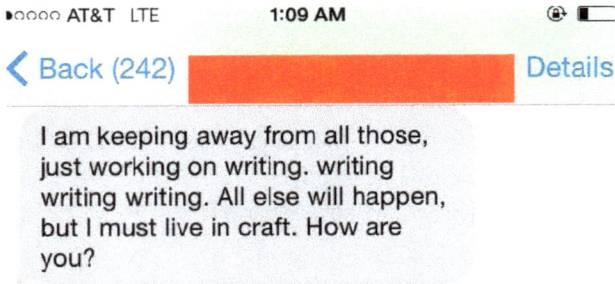

▸○○○○ AT&T LTE	1:09 AM	⊕ ▇
‹ Back (242)		**Details**

> I am keeping away from all those, just working on writing. writing writing writing. All else will happen, but I must live in craft. How are you?

[Collection of Evidence]

From the Desk of Title IX Coordinator O.

Continuation of Timeline of Events, According to Jane Doe's Initial Testimony

December, 18, 2013, ~3PM: During finals week, Doe allegedly receives a "desperate, out-of-the-blue" call from Professor X. asking her for a ride to the DMV, where he has an appointment to "finally get his driver's license."

December, 18, 2013, ~9:30 PM: Professor X. allegedly invites Doe over to his house for dinner and beers [reliable memory?] to "thank [Doe] for [her] help earlier that day." Doe and Professor X. allegedly end up "kissing and such" for an extended period of time in Professor X.'s kitchen.*

December, 18, 2013, ~11 PM: Professor X. allegedly asks Doe to temporarily leave his house because "Professor O. [of the Sociology Department] is supposed to stop by to retrieve his rabbit meat from the freezer [?] and it would not be very good if he walked in and saw [Doe] standing in the kitchen."

December 18, 2013, ~11PM – ~3AM: Doe goes to the library, where she attempts to finish the story she is due to submit to Professor X. the next day. She reports having a "very hard time focusing" on her academic work.

December, 18, 2013, ~3AM: Doe allegedly returns to Professor X.'s house to drive him to the airport, where he catches a transatlantic flight home for break.

* Note: when pressed, Doe refuses to elaborate on meaning of "and such"

●●●○○ AT&T LTE	1:42 AM	⊕ ▐▌
‹ Back (241)		Details

Thank you Sarah, much love and affection to you too. Have a beautiful day.

[Collection of Evidence]

Doe and Professor X. do not speak for the duration of break (almost six weeks) for reasons that, according to Doe, Professor X. later claims are due to his "limited internet connectivity" while overseas.

How do you write about something that isn't there?

He told me to start by writing about the spaces around the moment. "Write the gaps, and they will fill themselves in."

So I did—

I wrote about Navy blue sheets. The smells of salt and cheap cologne. Callouses. The light on the front porch of a house I couldn't leave. A swelling on my upper thigh. The grooves in the ceiling of my childhood bedroom. My fears of drowning, enclosed spaces, large hands, and other things capable of taking my breath away.

He handed me back my first draft with red lines through the margins. He continued to hand me back drafts marked in red throughout the upcoming months, as our meetings grew longer as, wordlessly, we transitioned from talking about the content on the pages in his office, to the picnic table behind the library, to the moonlit lounge of the little stone house, to the back of the little East Asian restaurant on the perimeters of the town: a place where People From the College Rarely Went—

Some of the sentences of the stories he'd return to me would be flanked by red brackets, like gates [this meant CUT]. Others would be circled and accentuated by two small checkmarks, emblems of approval.

He would talk about my writing using words that I could only describe as lovely—

Fragment. Disquiet. Ennui. Catharsis. Amnesia.

Words that said: *I want to help you tell your story.*

From the Desk of Title IX Coordinator O.

Preliminary Notes
Investigation into Misconduct Report Against X., Professor of Creative Writing
August 1, 2014

Continuation of Timeline of Events, according to Jane Doe's Initial testimony

Early February 2014: Upon returning to campus, Doe allegedly tries to get in touch with Professor X. through multiple outlets. He allegedly fails to respond for over a week. She starts to "grow anxious"— both confused about "where things stand between them" and worried because Professor X. is also supposed to advise the second half of her senior thesis project, a community-based visual storytelling project, which is scheduled to be publically displayed for the campus in less than a month. She needs his consent to receive academic credit for this endeavor.

Sarah Cheshire <sarah.n.cheshire@gmail.com>   2/2/14

I'm sorry if I'm bugging you. I hope you are well. I would really like to be able to talk to you sometime before classes start. All of a sudden I feel like I'm bearing the weight of a lot of things, regarding this school and the administration and the cnw department. It's a lot to hold and I'm having a really hard time figuring out who to trust. I really feel like I need your guidance before moving forward in the semester with a good conscience. I know you just got back but please let me know when you think you'll be settled in enough to check in

Best to you,

[Collection of Evidence]

Approx. February 8, 2014: Doe receives a generic

email from Professor X. addressed to herself and all of his other advisees, instructing them on how to sign up for fifteen-minute long beginning-of-semester "advising sessions." Doe responds to this email stating that, given "recent history," she would appreciate more than fifteen minutes of his time so that they can "both be on the same page moving forward into the upcoming semester." Professor X. responds three days later, stating that he has been "awfully busy with advising" but potentially has some room in his schedule tomorrow around 3:00 PM. Doe reports feeling "angry and confused" by this behavior. She also, however, knows that Professor X. has a history of migraines and that these sometimes cause him to "have a distorted sense of time and logic." She starts to construct a letter to him so that she can "clearly articulate" her thoughts when they meet [potential evidence?].

Approx. Feb 12, 2014: Professor X. and Doe allegedly convene at their "secret location" at his request. Professor X. allegedly gives Doe a hug, compliments her on her haircut and new tattoo. Doe states feeling as though they are "picking up right where the they off." At the end of the meeting, Doe allegedly asks Professor X. if he thinks that, given the "multiple roles they have recently assumed in each others' lives" and to avoid potential "conflicts of interest," it would be best for her to find a different advisor for her thesis project. She allegedly reads Professor X. her letter. Professor X. allegedly thanks her for her "beautiful, beautiful words." Responds that the decision of whether to switch advisors is "ultimately up to [her]" but he remains "deeply invested" in his role as her mentor and feels confident that "nothing about [his] commitment to this role has changed."

Professor X. allegedly tells Doe that he "thought of [her] often" while overseas, says "nothing inside of [him] regrets that kiss."

I understand the importance of respecting boundaries and formalities. I understand that we have to tread carefully. I am weighing these understandings against my need for accountability and openness. (but maybe these things are not mutually exclusive). I hope that you will try to be honest, even if it hurts me.

All of the bests to you,

Sarah

[Collection of Evidence]

Here's what I know to be true:

We were in his kitchen.

Even though it was five degrees outside, my hands were sweating profusely.

It was mid-December—December 18th, to be specific: three weeks after the snow began to fall, five months before the last patches of ice melted.

There were candles in the living room. There were empty glass bottles coated in wax lining the walls of his kitchen.

We had been drinking Angry Orchard cinnamon cider, which he had bought to thank me for spontaneously driving him to get his driver's license earlier that day.

At a little after 11:00 PM, he told me I should probably leave because he was scared that some other professor would stop by and see me there in his kitchen.

At around 3:00 AM, I returned to his house and frantically helped him clean his kitchen, then drove him to the airport. He was flying home for winter break, to a warm sunny place he claimed was filled with ghosts—

~~

[How was I to know that when he returned, he would no longer look me in the eye?]

From the Desk of Title IX Coordinator O.

Continuation of Timeline of Events, according to Jane Doe's Initial Testimony

Mid-Late February, 2014: Professor X. allegedly cancels four subsequent advising sessions with Doe. Doe experiences "increased panic" about fulfilling expectations for her senior project. Reports beginning to feel that "personal dynamics might be effecting professional rapport" between herself and Professor X.

March 1, 2014: Doe's storytelling installation begins to receive campus-wide recognition as she accumulates over 300 story submissions from students, faculty members, custodial staff, community members, etc. Professor X. is asked to give a statement to a student publication about the project. Allegedly speaks to how "deeply proud" he is of how Doe's creative work has matured under the auspices of his mentorship.

Here's what I know to be true:

March 4, 2014: Professor X. allegedly shows up at the Convocation Hall just in time to see Doe's display being broken down and packed.

From: Sarah Cheshire <   >
Date: Tue, 4 Mar 2014 12:18:15 -0500
To: >
Subject: Important

Come to   ASAP, even if only for 2 minutes! Important beautiful thing happening

On Tuesday, March 4, 2014, Sarah Cheshire -   ~ wrote:
   Hurryhrryhurry it's only happening for ten more mins

   On Tuesday, March 4, 2014, Sarah Cheshire ~   ~ wrote:
      Hurry ! :)

      On Tuesday, March 4, 2014, Sarah Cheshire ·   ~ wrote:
      Oh well.
      When you get the chance also please respond to my email from this morning

[Collection of evidence]

Between leaving and returning to his kitchen, I trudged through the gaunt snow to the library and spread loose pages across my cubicle—

March 6th, 2014: Doe texts Professor X. expressing a desire to debrief her project. Professor X. responds that he is "very busy meeting with students" but can possibly schedule time "from 2:00 – 2:30 PM every other Thursday." Doe reports starting to have fleeting moments of "disorientation" and "constriction of breath."

[Tried to read through the blur of his scrawl over my text. Tried to parse words from words. Tried to hush the

lingering friction of hands on skin long enough to fill the gaps in the story I had been trying all semester to tell—]

Approx. March 12. 2014: Doe and Professor X. go on a long walk on the outskirts of campus. He allegedly tells her she is beautiful. They allegedly make plans to go on a roadtrip together after graduation, agree that pursuing anything before then is "too dangerous."

> *I was leaning against the stove,*
> *He was leaning against the stove,*

Approx. March 13, 2014: Doe receives series of "flattering" text messages from Professor X., highlighting his "profound care" for her, her work, and her presence in his life.

Mid March, 2014: Professor E. continues to email Doe from private account, urging her to remain cautious about whom she talks with about "anything involving Professor X."

One of us was leaning against the stove, which was underneath the only window in his kitchen.

Late March, 2014: Doe reports experiencing increasing paranoia that the college administration is 'surveilling' her and Professor X. Worries consistently that someone "will find out about what happened in his kitchen in December" or that she "will accidentally say the wrong thing to the wrong person and all of [her] organizing work will be discredited and [she] will [expletive] everything up" [Doe's words].

[I remember how the metal handle kneaded into my lower back]
He was facing the window—
[I remember looking over his shoulder at the withered rosemary plant on the windowsill]
I was facing the window—

Mid-afternoon, Approx. April 4, 2014: A friend of Doe's allegedly sees a listing for a newly created Creative Writing tenure track faculty position on the college's Human Resources webpage, emails Doe to congratulate her on the success of her organizing. Doe reports "feeling taken off guard" by this. Contacts

Professor E. via secret email account. Professor E. confirms the creation of this position.

to █████ me ▾

The letter of appointment has gone out: it's official. ████ has now been appointed to a tenure track position in Creative Writing.

--

You don't know till you find out.

[Collection of Evidence]

~~

[How is it that I've come to hold two contradictory memories at once?]

From the Desk of Title IX Coordinator O.

Continuation of Timeline of Events, according to Jane Doe's Initial Testimony

Sometime around April 4, 2014, approx. 5 PM: Doe texts Professor X. congratulating him on his new job and asking why, "given all of [her] work towards getting the position created," she was not informed when her efforts came into fruition. Professor X. responds: I have no knowledge of the things you are talking about and I would encourage you not to make note of this to anyone. Doe asks for clarification, wondering if she's "done something wrong" [reports feeling "Jedi Mind-Tricked"]. Professor X. responds: you have done nothing wrong. Continue studying and enjoying your senior year, and try not to think or talk about these matters. Doe asks Professor X. to meet as soon he can, stating that she feels "someone owes [her] an explanation." Professor X. responds: I am very very busy with class prep tonight and tomorrow but don't think too much about this. It is nothing you should be concerning yourself with; you have done good work. Doe replies: "all of this is suddenly making me feel like I am going crazy." Gets no response.

[Collection of Evidence]

I said I shouldn't be here. He said, you shouldn't be here— I leaned back, he leaned in. He leaned back, I leaned in—

Sometime around April 4, 2014, approx. 8:30 PM: Doe allegedly bumps into a fellow Creative Writing student in the library, who informs her "jovially" that he has just returned from getting drinks with Professor X. at the campus bar to "discuss his thesis."

Sometime around April 4, 2014, approx. 8:45 PM: Doe has "panic attack" in Sylvia Plath section of the college library. Reports suddenly becoming overcome by a feeling that "she can no longer recognize or trust her surroundings," accompanied by "acute dizziness and a loss of breath."

Sometime around April 4, 2014, approx. 10 PM: Doe emails Professor X., copying Professor E., stating feelings that she is being "used and disrespected" and that "her reality is somehow being distorted." Says she wants to know why "people are suddenly withholding truth" from her. Threatens to publically withdraw support for Professor X.'s petition if he doesn't respond.

~~We were his hand, my hipbone. We were my hipbone,~~
~~his hand—~~
~~We were his hum, my giggle. We were my giggle, his~~
~~thigh—~~

Sometime around April 4, 2014, approx. 11 PM: Professor X. emails Doe asking her to meet him in his office.

[We were thigh to thigh]

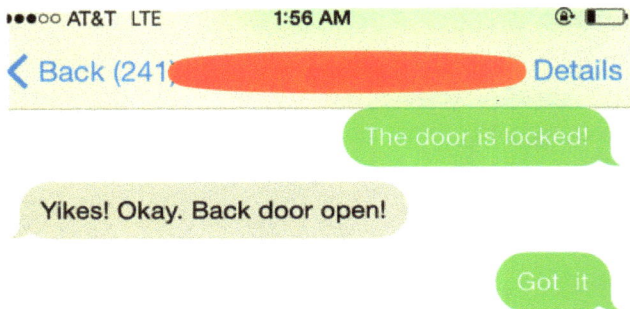

[Collection of Evidence]

Sometime around April 4, 2014, approx. 11:20 PM:
Doe and Professor X. allegedly hold hands in the lounge of the stone house. He tells her that he is still concerned that his "enemies in the college" will find ways to undermine his newly created tenure track position, that he fears that there isn't sufficient time to renew his visa. He claims he withheld information from Doe earlier because he wanted to "spare her the drama." He allegedly tells her how much he cares about her and how grateful he is for all she has done.

We were my lips to his lips, we were his lips to my lips—
[We were breath to breath]

Sometime around April 4, 2014, approx. 12:20 AM: Doe finds herself "apologizing to Professor X." for "acting crazy." They embrace.

Sometime around April 4, 2014, approx. 1:00 AM: Professor X. allegedly rises suddenly, claiming he hears footsteps. Doe hides in the basement of the Creative Writing House then flees out the backdoor into the melting snow, leaving her coat behind.

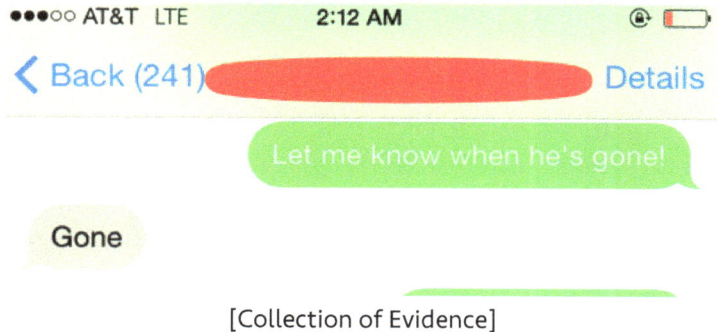

●●●○○ AT&T LTE	2:12 AM	🔒 ▭
‹ Back (241)	████████████	Details

Let me know when he's gone!

Gone

[Collection of Evidence]

~~*We were his body to mine, his body to mine, his body to mine, my body to—*~~
[We were body to body, that night in his kitchen]

Mid April, 2014: A campus newspaper contacts Doe for an interview re: the newly created tenure track position, asking her to speak about "why she is so inspired by Professor X.'s teaching." Professor E. calls Doe to review interview etiquette.

Sarah,

Good. Please don't feel bad....but don't trust. And know that they are making you feel powerful because they see you as a useful source of information. I include the Dean of STudents in that. Also, ▮▮▮ was probably coming on to you. I'm presently working on the position request and letter of support for ▮▮▮ send to ▮▮ and CFC. Fingers crossed....but the donor has already sent the check supporting the position....so even though things can still go wrong.... I'm hopeful.

BTW, I have heard further collaboration for the story that that ▮▮▮ had been appointed because of students rallying to his support.

[Collection of Evidence]

Mid April, 2014: Professor X. allegedly "falls off the face of the planet" for 10 days. Fails to show up to his classes, misses meetings, etc. Doe emails him asking if he is okay and if there is anything more he needs from her re: her senior project. Receives no response.

Up until that night in his kitchen, skin was the only thing upholding the boundary between us: separating the appropriate from the inappropriate, the yes from the no, the discreet from the tangible. Before that night, we could dwell in the spaces between lines, defined by intuition and exchanges of imprecise words. We could speak in metaphor about the rooms we hovered at the thresholds of, gazed into through frosted windows, but never entered—

●●○○ AT&T LTE   1:51 AM   ⊕ ▭

❮ Back (241) ▬▬▬▬▬▬▬▬▬   Details

> Hey hey it's raining, any thoughts on a backup location?

Perhaps tomorrow may be a better day to meet Sarah, the rain is coming down quite hard now & tomorrow may work better weather-wise. I'm suggesting we mee

t at 4:30 tomorrow if it still works for you? Behind the yellow house or perhaps the public library garden?

> I can't meet tomorrow in the afternoon. I have a lesson planning meeting for my job. I'm sorry. Is there any chance you could still do this afternoon? Public library?

I got rained on pretty badly just now and won't be venturing out ▬▬▬

●●○○○ AT&T LTE   2:03 AM   ⊕ ▭

❮ Back (241) ▬▬▬▬▬▬▬▬▬   Details

> To be honest, I also went out in the rain to meet you ▬▬▬▬▬▬

[Collection of Evidence]

Late April, 2014: Professor X. reemerges. He and Doe allegedly meet at "secret location." He tells her that indeed the tenure track position was not created in time for him to renew his work visa, that he might have to return to his home country for a year and has been in a "very, very bad mental place" about it. They hold hands and talk more about his anxieties and their upcoming roadtrip—

But as soon as our skin touched, we crossed a line, stepped into a forbidden room, did the thing we knew couldn't be undone; he crossed a line, did the thing he knew couldn't be undone with words—

Early May, 2014: Professor X. disappears again.

*[We were his flesh to my flesh
We were my flesh to his flesh]*

May 19, 2014: Two days after final semester grades are due—three days before graduation—Professor X. allegedly approaches Doe as she is walking across the quad with friends, en route to a senior celebration. Professor X. asks to speak with Doe alone. He tells her that her senior thesis display in March was "unequivocally of A+ quality" but "unfortunately" she never turned in the "reflection paper that was supposed to accompany it" and therefore he is "forced to lower her grade to an A-." Then, he walks away.

We were flesh to flesh, that night in his kitchen—
Everything else is subject to interpretation.

From the Desk of Title IX Coordinator O.

Preliminary Notes
Investigation into Misconduct Report Against X., Professor of Creative Writing
September 16, 2014

Professor X.'s Testimony

September 16, 2014: Title IX Coordinator O. calls Professor X. into her office. Relays Doe's accounts of what happened between her and him during the 2013–2014 academic year. Asks for his perspective on the matter at hand.

Professor X. responds: "I know nothing of the stories she is telling."

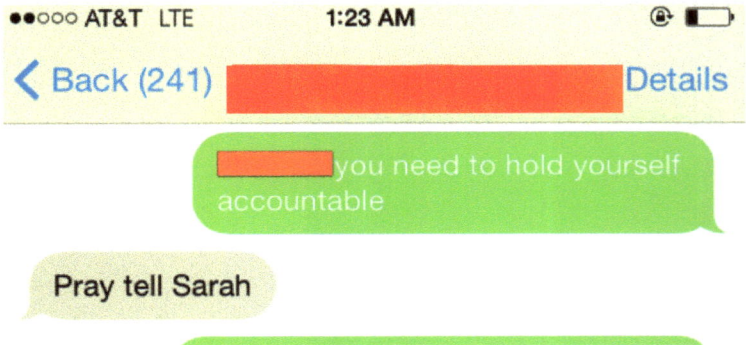

●●○○○ AT&T LTE   1:23 AM

‹ Back (241)   Details

███████ you need to hold yourself accountable

Pray tell Sarah

[Collection of Evidence]

"He knows nothing of the stories you are telling," she tells me on the phone as I crouch under the green awning of a block-like office building on K Street, itching holes into the seams of my stockings.

It is six weeks after the night at that bar, nine months since that night in his kitchen. I've recently moved to D.C. for an office job at a non-profit, where I spend nine hours a day softening stiff legal jargon into words that the average person might be able to understand. It's a city of sharp angles, straight lines, and men with firm handshakes and shifty eyes. I constantly feel like a round peg in a square hole, in my ripped tights and mismatched socks and constant confusion of *networking* with *making friends*, a social faux-pas which, years later, I realize is rooted in a history of having *professional* and *personal* lines blurred. My friends tell me to fake it 'til you make it, as if taming the ghosts under my skin is a simple matter of willpower and freshly-ironed pencil skirts.

~~

I left the small town in the midwest but, in the small room with the crimson armchair, the investigation went on without me: "We have an obligation to make the school a safe learning environment for students."

~~

How do you write about something that isn't there?

~~

Months later, I will attempt to recount the sequence of events to a therapist in Silver Spring: *Snowstorm. Kitchen. Red marker. Clammy hands. The absence of Mother. "Disquiet, Nonlinear, Pedestrian." A kiss that became a story of a kiss. A misplaced touch. The feeling of skin unraveling.* She will hover her pen over her yellow legal pad and squint. "It's awful how he took advantage of you like that."

I will leave the room and not come back.

~~

After all the facts were documented, I asked the Title IX Coordinator—maybe begged her—to allow for an informal investigation. "I don't want anyone to get in trouble. It was just as much me as it was him—" The informal process would have resulted in mediation rather than punitive measures, determined by a weighing of facts and evidence. Ideally, through mediation, I would tell my story, he would tell his, and we would meet somewhere in the middle.

"It was complicated, you see—"

~~

[We were flesh to flesh, that night in his kitchen—]

~~

I pull a loose thread from a fray in the knee of my tights. The hole begins to widen into a chasm—

~~

"I know nothing of the stories she is telling"

~~

I brace myself for the familiar unraveling: the air being sucked out of my lungs, the layers of touches charging up through my flesh—

But instead, for a brief moment, I find myself back in his office, October, 2013:

It is a gentle day: not *muted*, just soft. The snow still buried somewhere in the pewter sky, the frigid Lake Erie winds suspended. A breeze tousling the red tips of the oak tree outside the window. Words, like leaves, tumbling from our mouths with a beautifully imprecise grace. Him, looking at me in a prolonged silence: not yet *disquiet*, just quiet—

I want to help you tell your stories.

And me, holding my breath, the story on my lap still unmarked by his red pen—

~~

I didn't want to punish him. To punish him would be to punish myself: *I wanted to be there just as much as he did, right?*

I just wanted resolve. Reconciliation. Maybe even a rekindling of something. What he called *restorative justice*. A tighter ending: not the one in which I stand gaping on the campus quad days before graduation as he walks away.

I assumed that, when he stepped into the Title IX Office, our stories would converge; if not in details, at least in the events that took place in his kitchen. Or in the simple fact that we were there, after dark, that evening in December 2013—

Maybe this is where I was naïve all along—

We both knew that the story of what happened between us was complex and imprecise, as well-told stories tend to be. I wanted badly to believe that we could come to terms with it as such. Regardless of the nuances of our memories, I wanted to believe in the story itself. After all, we were never supposed to be arbitrators, right?

Finding a singular truth. that was the realm of academics and lawyers and K Street lobbyists. But we were storytellers. And as storytellers, our job was never to dichotomize the world into parallel lines of black and white but to figure out how to dwell in the spaces between the lines: those murky, abstract, unstable spaces some might define as *grey*. The spaces of the gut—

I wanted to believe that we were fumbling through these spaces together, walking weightlessly through the snow, meeting in secret rooms, leaning into those boundaries deemed *inappropriate*, prodding the *disquiet*—

But he outmaneuvered me.

With one swift sentence, he struck a red line through all the words I'd spilled on the floor in front of us—

I know nothing of the stories she is telling.

Acknowledgements

My Deepest Gratitude:

To Michael Martone's Fall 2016 Hypoxic Workshop at the University of Alabama for supporting and challenging me in my process of writing this piece.

To my Oberlin College Dialogue Center community, who provided the framework for how I continue to engage in the process of storytelling.

To the women of my undergrad years (plus Jesse, Max, and Ethan) who refused to let me fall. You are all my muses.

To Rashné for inspirational sticky notes, midnight drives to Lake Erie, and helping me learn to sit with myself.

To Davi, who shares my appreciation of the absurd and is never afraid to tell it like it is.

To Meredith, Eric, and Monique who never doubted my story. I've never known anyone who brings humanity to administrative work like y'all do.

To Lexie for lantern tattoos and ghost stories.

To Tom for showing me that love can be honest.

And to Lynn Powell, who embodies the kinds of wisdom, compassion, intentionality and effervescent curiosity I strive towards every day. You inspire me to continue to write.

Thank you, thank you.

Colophon

The front cover text, title page, and page numbers are set in DJB Chalk It Up.

The back cover text is set in Seravek.

The body text is set in STIXGeneral.

The Title IX Coordinator reports are set in Seravek, with Myanmar MN for the running head and Veteran Typewriter for the heading information.

All other headers are set in Admiration Pains.

Front and back matter are set in Seravek.

Sarah Cheshire is an MFA student in prose at the University of Alabama, where she also serves as a nonfiction editor for the *Black Warrior Review*. Her writing has appeared in the 2014 Anthology *Southern Sin: True Stories of the Sultry South and Women Behaving Badly* (InFact Books), on pbs.org, and forthcoming in *Scalawag Magazine*. A native North Carolinian, she feels most at home amidst oak trees, bluegrass music, and her rescue mutt, Dolly Parsnip.

Etchings Press

Etchings Press is a student-run publisher at the University of Indianapolis. Each year, student editors choose the Whirling Prize, a post-publication award, in the fall and coordinate a publication contest for one poetry chapbook, one prose chapbook, and one novella in the spring. For more information, please visit etchings. uindy.edu.

Previous winners and publications

Poetry
2019: *As Lovers Always Do* by Marne Wilson
2018: *In the Herald of Improbable Misfortunes* by Robert Campbell
2017: *Uncle Harold's Maxwell House Haggadah* by Danny Caine
2016: *Some Animals* by Kelli Allen
2015: *Velocity of Slugs* by Joey Connelly
2014: *Action at a Distance* by Christopher Petruccelli

Prose
2019: *Dissenting Opinion from the Committee
        for the Beatitudes* by Marc J. Sheehan (fiction)
2018: *The Forsaken* by Chad V. Broughman (fiction)
2017: *Unravelings* by Sarah Cheshire (memoir)
2016: *Pathetic* by Shannon McLeod (essays)
2015: *Ologies* by Chelsea Biondolillo (essays)
2014: *Static: Stories* by Frederick Pelzer (fiction)

Novella
2019: *Savonne, Not Vonny* by Robin Lee Lovelace
2018: *Edge of the Known Bus Line* by James R. Gapinski
2017: *The Denialist's Almanac of American Plague and
        Pestilence* by Christopher Mohar
2016: *Followers* by Adam Fleming Petty